# Illuminated Edges

# Illuminated Edges

Poems by

Adam Day

© 2024 Adam Day. All rights reserved.
This material may not be reproduced in any form, published,
reprinted, recorded, performed, broadcast,
rewritten, or redistributed without
the explicit permission of Adam Day.
All such actions are strictly prohibited by law.

Cover image by The Rubin Museum
Author photo by Michael Winters

ISBN: 978-1-63980-572-3

Kelsay Books
502 South 1040 East, A-119
American Fork, Utah 84003
Kelsaybooks.com

*What elegy is, not loss but opposition.*
—C. D. Wright

# Acknowledgments

Thank you to the following publications, in which versions of these poems previously appeared:

*Antiserious:* "Extraneous Copper," "Being Alive May Come in Use"
*Barrow Street:* "Evacuating Liberty or We'll Make a Man of You, and a Woman"
*Bayou:* "On the Bicentennial"
*Birdcoat Quarterly:* "Bricolage"
*The Boiler:* "Cynanthropy"
*Boston Review:* "Father Benides"
*Cimarron:* "Moth Among the Tits"
*Cold Front:* "*Heimweh* Funicular"
*The Collagist:* "What Would I Document?"
*Descant:* "Nothing's Branch," "Translocation"
*Diagram:* "You Can Get Used to Almost Anything," "Letters from Shore"
*Diode:* "Love Letter from Edda Görring"
*Grist:* "I Shall Be Sent for Soon"
*The Inflectionist:* "A Kind of Speech," "Elegy," "Aubade," "An Ending," "A Bodily Way of Knowing," "Shared Breath," "Elegy II"
*Interrupture:* "Low Tide"
*The Journal:* "Running Off at the Mouth," "Bricolage II"
*Makeout Creek:* "Accept the World and Go to Parties"
*Maximus:* "Monkey's Mind," "Rehabilitation," "Redoubt"
*Meridian:* "Equus," "Love Letter Penned in a *Pissoire*"
*Miniskirt:* "A Method"
*Oyster River Pages:* "One Truth of Caring"
*Poetry New Zealand:* "White Clouds in Dark Valleys"
*Poetry Online:* "Écouter"
*Prelude:* "Geography and Customs"

*Queen Mob's Tea:* "And Children Were Regarded with Suspicion"
*So and So:* "Ihre Kinder"
*Softblow:* "Our Polyphemus"
*South Florida Poetry Journal:* "Mosaic"
*Tirage Monthly:* "Apprehended at a Distance"
*Tusculum Review:* "The Quiet Life"
*Under a Warm Green Linden:* "A Movement"
*The Volta (They Will Sew the Blue Sail):* "We Must Get You Interested in a Girl"
*Word Riot:* "Destination"

The following poems first appeared in the chapbook, *Badger, Apocrypha*—usually under titles other than those they appear under in this collection—published as part of the Poetry Society of America's Chapbook Fellowship series: "And Children Were Regarded with Suspicion," "Running Off at the Mouth."

Some Poems appeared in the chapbook collection, *Nothing's Branch*, published by Bottlecap Press.

# Contents

| | |
|---|---|
| Father Benides | 13 |
| Running off at the Mouth | 14 |
| A Method | 15 |
| Geography and Customs | 16 |
| Low Tide | 17 |
| We Must Get You Interested in a Girl | 19 |
| Rehabilitation | 20 |
| Redoubt | 21 |
| Equus | 22 |
| Mosaic | 23 |
| I Shall Be Sent for Soon | 24 |
| You Can Get Used to Almost Anything | 25 |
| Extraneous Copper | 27 |
| Cynanthropy | 28 |
| Apprehended at a Distance | 29 |
| A Movement | 30 |
| Ihre Kinder | 31 |
| *Heimweh* Funicular | 32 |
| White Clouds in Dark Valleys | 33 |
| Nothing's Branch | 34 |
| Love Letter Penned in a *Pissoire* | 36 |
| Moth Among the Tits | 38 |
| What Would I Document? | 40 |
| *Écouter* | 41 |
| Rodan | 42 |
| La Ci Darem | 44 |
| Our Polyphemus | 45 |
| And Children Were Regarded with Suspicion | 46 |
| Pillars Of | 47 |
| Destination | 48 |
| Monkey Mind | 49 |
| Accept the World and Go to Parties | 51 |
| Letters from the Shore | 52 |

| | |
|---|---:|
| Evacuating Liberty or We'll Make a Man of You, and a Woman | 53 |
| On the Bicentennial | 55 |
| The Quiet Life | 56 |
| Love Letter from Edda Göring | 59 |
| Bricolage II | 64 |
| A Kind of Speech | 65 |
| Elegy | 66 |
| Aubade | 67 |
| One Truth of Caring | 68 |
| Being Alive May Come in Use | 70 |
| An Ending | 71 |
| A Bodily Way of Knowing | 72 |
| Shared Breath | 74 |
| Elegy II | 76 |
| Translocation | 77 |
| Bricolage | 78 |

# Father Benides

Father Benides touched me in my special

place when I was eight. Then he put
his little man—like the neck of a goose

tethered to a telephone pole—to my forehead.
Families locked away in their houses—

drained swimming pools, deserted
runways, the flooded river. Everyone

is the way they are. I think
I laughed—as if I knew where I was

going, as if my shadow jogged on
before me. It's not well to laugh

at another man's misfortune. Father
Benides only smoothed my hair—I stared

at the chips in the ceiling. My conscience
is clear as regards having done

my duty. It's his anger I envy most
today; his anger and his directness.

# Running off at the Mouth

There are no Siamese twins in this
town, no albinos; only soccer

matches, bourbon, steaming horses
and the slick skirts of afterbirth hanging

from hind-ends. I don't care how
depressed you are, I'm not coming

to your party. Champagne
and sodomy are overrated—in that order.

Smoking in the shower, with a bacon
sandwich and a boy named Daniel waiting

on the sink, on the other hand, are
supremely underrated. I admit,

I'm an unnecessarily handsome
knockabout, nightly drunk to no apparent

effect. But, it's nice to be worried about.
It's almost like being cared about.

# A Method

Nothing pushes
Steve and I away

from each other,
as I wipe the city's

moisture from his face,
the dark thoughts

surrounded by neon
in Union Square

cutting through
falling flakes. And

he brushes the snow
off of my shoulders,

and my fingers become
breathless. When this poem

is over we're going
to get high together,

we're going to go
to a movie together.

# Geography and Customs

I wasn't a very good student in bed; just
sort of got by. Mine was a passion
which both enveloped a beloved and didn't
have much to do with her. But
as so often when you exhibit reluctance
to do something, people think you must be
very good at it. I can only hope
that even if it was boring that
was interesting too. I wonder how things
happened that way for me. I'm not the person
who knows. I can't seem to find anything
that's an example of what I mean: It's so wonderful
to be back in France. But I hate *ze French!*

# Low Tide

My dear
David, I see

no one, suddenly,
neither women

nor stallions.
I have no

idea how long
it will drag on.

I used to enjoy
Maddy, but her allusiveness

poses a challenge.
I spoke

with Michael
and liked him

but he is defeated.
Willful seclusion

is, I suppose,
the measure

of dirty habits—
the little cormorant

plunge of voracious
curiosity into

a wan, gritty
anus. But look—

the sun, forgetting
to be wretched,

has taken it
into its head

to bare its bottom
over my green eaves.

# We Must Get You Interested in a Girl

Autumnal horseflies fabricate
fornications 'round cracked
streetlamps throwing cold light
before fistfuls of rain,
and the hickory trees in panic.
Inside, more serious than I,
you'd have remained in bed
for a period of twenty years,
a body at loss of definition,
and shot nerves, under the gaze
of pale-skinned young nurses,
the smell of mold rising
from the floor. Formerly little more
than a succession of local
phenomenon—like feet growing
accustomed to the dark—
you are the bloodiest Christ,
trundling off to the cultural center
with a projector
under one arm—we must
get you interested in a girl,
a friend who might do
all things for you, front to back.
Only, I might have done them better.

# Rehabilitation

My aunt shaves
in her underwear

while she talks
to her hair—like

plant sentience:
"If you leave

someone, you've
got to do it

for a real
piece of ass."

The whole thing
is ridiculous:

it's like being
inside a bird;

where do you
live when

you're sick?

# Redoubt

Night mountain
snow is unlike
them living
inside his head:

There is one less
table setting.
He had nothing

to fear, though
he went in fear—
there was nothing

they could do
to him, or
very little.

# Equus

About the horses,
we strangled them
because we loved them,
unstrangled because
we despised them,
sucking the sweat
from our lips, theirs,
darkness behind us,
in the ice-plated
watermeadow and purple
cabbage, to have them
again pull us
from the place
we galloped
ourselves into.

# Mosaic

A man enters
a tree cavity,

a foot through
the floorboard

of desire, mouth filled
with concrete,

sockets with moss;
rose-colored snakes

to sew the ribs
together. Mind

not striving. Hand
out to feed black

catbirds; transients.
Warm shadow

catching up
all that light.

# I Shall Be Sent for Soon

I will, in the end, marry
myself. Lecherous
as a macaque.
Ungovernable
tongue. Performance
outliving desire. My eyes
are tired of myself.
A sow in a suit
of armor. Feral dove.
Performing old sins
in new ways.

# You Can Get Used to Almost Anything

I'm a lamb, a baby's
passed gas, a cock

like a fish
holding its head

out of water,
eyes

of a pregnant cat,
shirtless with suspenders

clipped to briefs,
I've drawn a circle

around myself.
I'll try to make

my face laugh: I eat
wax fruit

because I never
quite love what I love.

So, I don't go into town
very often anymore—

instead it's the ballgame
on TV, trying

to meditate panic
flat, or screwing

anyway
someone who licks

my face away, half
or twice my age

I already knew
I didn't want.

# Extraneous Copper

Would you like to be friends, one
adult asks another. Aren't ordinary
troubles enough? Don't worry too much
what the neighbor thinks. He's a fucking great
teddy bear. Then again, one doesn't want
one's name in her majesty's guestbook,
come the revolution. But will they
remember and talk about the soft skin
over my calves like blue honey
dusk. The way space is depicted
as a reflection of how we behave
in space. Tea service with sea swells
behind. I will love you at 8 p.m. next Tuesday.

# Cynanthropy

The citizen's daughter
sleepwalked

into his room. Thinking
her his wife

come back,
and pleased to see

the spirit
of improvisation

alive and well,
he gave himself

to her. Soft hand
under a hen. Next

morning they
could be heard

saying
to one another,

"What are you
laughing at?"

# Apprehended at a Distance

*After Lauren Berlant*


Disintegrated silence. Goes
without saying, yet fails
to reach meaning. A shrug,
an absurd onward.
In life without wanting
the world—things don't
add up, but are in range.
I am sexually incoherent
and lack rhythm; I am
apprehended at a distance.
You are a thing for others—
give a gift. I was in that
thing—history in modes
of coping, bodily habits.
I miss your mechanical
attention. I subtract parts
of myself—now it, and it,
less I, without ceasing
to exist, commentary without
counterforce. Still, I should
like to be found well-composed
and wearing my glasses.

# A Movement

*After Joe Wenderoth*


Stop everything and wait.
You're almost there.

Agony is wherever. Agony
is not like anything.

Not thunder eating
the sleep of mice.

Not quite heavy snow falling
on a burning house.

# Ihre Kinder

There's no new apple, unisexed, no
new metal, only a disappearing
         vocabulary and correspondence—
         the earth having thrown us
running unbuttoned, back to cracked

         caves and turlygod, to keep
         and sleep in earthen
basements unarchitected, beyond a little fire
in a field, and the white-haired waves

pinioning terns—we throw our heads at them.

## *Heimweh* Funicular

It was not
the socialism

we dreamt of:
principled but allowing

for private
bourgeois niceties—

as for living, our servants
can do that for us. We are

consigned, without
remedy; going somewhere—

almost: the moon
boom-hinged

to an oil rig. The printer
apologized for two weeks, day

and night. Whenever
a box of paper ran

out, the computer
displayed the number

of times it had apologized—
if not good,

then careful, like the girl beneath
harbor lights shining

like satellites; the father
who is not great, but fine.

# White Clouds in Dark Valleys

What it was—I lost my brother
at the garden gate. They came
for him, the wood foxes with tilted
gray caps. We had wondered
when it would begin. I took my hands
from my pockets. The others
stood at the window. We couldn't
quite go after him. All night
we talked. They put him in a bin
over there, his one clonic hand
hanging from its metal mouth,
the rest of him only interior shadow.

# Nothing's Branch

There are wicked tricks
in this life, said the rooster,

dismounting the duck,
which is to say the streets

have changed, but I'm
still the same, which is

to say, screw you Gloria,
I'm not a goddamn

son of a bitch. I am depressed,
of course, or if death

is a long sleep then I'm
damn tired. I lack the courage

to slip the cliff and still
somehow night never goes

quickly enough. I am
no longer the man

I fell in love with. I'd like
to have been born wearing spats

and a dickey, already towering,
gnawing squares of broken crockery

and cherry blossoms. I'd like
to play at being the bakery's

scrolling security door, or the kind
of woman a man might need,

hips like Cinderella, and wander
about in the thickets

of inelegant freedom.

## Love Letter Penned in a *Pissoire*

Little heart
of snow


that can find
no rest


on her bed
of down. Fricatrix


squatting on moss,
collapsing on


the banquet, don't-
give-a-damn-ish. My


bitch of a heart,
drifting whoral


toward a conveniently
remote accessibility.


Why can't I
tell you

what I feel
without getting


on a platform,
or wet? Be a bear,


a sycamore. I never
think of you. I


never do.

# Moth Among the Tits

Maybe you know things

    I don't; worst of all, someone

like you, deserted side street,

incompetent, but kind stage prop

    or porter. Nothing sensible

to say, and on we go, just the same,

for who cares. And the difference

    between whose hand is held or hits,

yours or some other's? Though

just once I would have liked

    to submit. Won't you be my little

godsend I wondered,

to wander beneath the alders together

    without being shat upon by the ghetto

of starlings? Overwilling to kneel

and gawp, you demand

    a cock among the does, a moth

among the tits, rarely doing

but being done to, like a bladder,

    purpose of which is be filled up

and emptied, in which, as in nothing other,

you found fidelity to self-mutilation,

    like monkey's eyes which think

there is something beyond, and sad

or angry, cannot get at it.

# What Would I Document?

If you'd known
what a bland man

I was
when you married me

I could have
avoided all those

emotional crises.
But what's wrong

with being slapped?
I request it.

And there is
the sound of water

spilling down
the back of the desk.

I am
an aardvark-tongued

bootlicker, but
for a long time

there weren't
any witnesses.

# *Écouter*

*After Michael Dickman and Joe Wenderoth*

It is not in your power
to slow down. It is not

in your power to choose
the road. Your power

(if you'd like to call it that)
is to choose the songs

between now and the wreck.
They sound the same,

the living and the dead.
To tell them apart, I have to

listen so closely. I have to
remember what I know.

Their mansions of snow,
barkdust, gnats, and sunlight.

# Rodan

You are someone who thinks
that because they talk often

about their emotions
they understand them. You clasp an elm

holding the place where someone else
had been. Thousands of miles away

we're doing the same thing
and it looks nothing alike. If you just

threaten the pipes with a hammer
the water at least will come. It was

suicide to be abroad—a long time
I wondered how I might do it; unhinge

the wrist where it wrinkles and let go.
But what was it to be at home,

Mrs.? A lingering dissolution? The methodical
decomposition of a stunningly odd

composite? Like the sandhills
of my belly. The high grass

bends beneath them. I'm hung
like a baby carrot and a couple of *petits pois,*

while your embonpoint has ridden
to the field. Your mind

is a town no one visits; like loneliness,
it endangers libraries. At first I wanted to sleep

with your sisters; by the end I wanted
to sleep with your mother. I don't know

what's beyond that stand
of trees or what's keeping it.

## La Ci Darem

Let's be grown up
children growing

back down, guilty
persons playing

at being guilty—you
can learn the role

backstage; I'll bite
your ankles. Jailbirds

with keyholes; queens
with prize bulls;

in slumbering summer
fields. Ripening the cervix

with a boiled owl, *sur
la mer*. Hand

at the throat. A come cry
shoved back in

like swimming
handcuffed—roof

of the mouth, oh
boy! Lovely

weather
we're having.

# Our Polyphemus

He was born,
his little paws

fumbling the air
for purchase,

and we took
a look

at his overcast
cock and said,

"A bit
off the top."

# And Children Were Regarded with Suspicion

*With lines from Bonnie 'Prince' Billy*

He is the first shit of the fourth
    reich, in yellow galoshes. Gelding

a horse called Palestrina, has the expression
    of an intelligent dog. Unreliable witness

to his own existence—he moves like
    a mistake; his buttock celebrates

itself. He slit his right wrist like drawing
    a watch from a pocket. Like coughing.

Above the shadow of the valley
    of the kitchen sink, singing, "I'm

afeared if I don't have a piglet, lamb,
    or little calf I'll chop my humanness

in half," like twisting a doorknob
    in a night-quiet room where two sleep

furled, and sleep, and are unaware.

# Pillars Of

Neighbors brought news
of an attack. The hair was stapled

to the headboard. We wondered
if they had hands; tongues

were found—a kind
of penance, we thought. More

than one. There were hoof-prints
in the morning mud.

The umbrella was still
in its stand. It was bored

with itself—it will not talk. Which,
of course, may be very kind,

considering.

# Destination

*After Franz Kafka*

I cram them
all into

the drawer
I am there

too and then
wait then

open it
a little

to see
if all have

suffocated
if not

close the drawer
again, and go

on like this
to the end.

# Monkey Mind

Shotgun my brain

and tendons into words

onto the wall. The trigger-digit

sings though

it doesn't feel

its best. It should be

ashamed; people will

be mad—them do moral

history. But screw Jack

and sister and Santa

and sir! This island feels

less and more about less. But

if I escape to Montana,

Slovenia? All did or are doing:

thrive, nervous hurts—then

the appointment—forty years long

enough in a taxi

going home? One day

I will rope with my own

hands or dive into schist—

forget footnotes

and news and truth. Take

a word for it. My mind

is fine. The jerk.

# Accept the World and Go to Parties

I wish I were
god in Mainz

annulled in beer
growing old

in the shadow
of compromise

working back
from cruelty

to original sin.

# Letters from the Shore

I have to write you. You
will not go away. It isn't

true love. The true
love will be another. But

we'll come to that
later. I hope. Cruelty's

not local; stay home.
The beaches

photogenically desolate;
curated shoals

of calcified fish and plover
bones—the country's load

of manure and ton
of bricks. Grey gulls

nailed to the wind,
French-fries clenched

in their bills.
Aren't people

shits. Never do
quite what you ask them.

# Evacuating Liberty
## or We'll Make a Man of You, and a Woman


Sticking your head
      out the train window
like drinking a cup

of cold tea,
      like a commodity
designed to stimulate

desire and impulse
      into reality, a conduit
for teaching

cleanliness on the heels
      of chaos, lively
as a long yawn,

a good portrait
      of furniture,
long periods

of tedium punctuated
      by moments
of terror, shortage

of bathrooms,
      the mother duck
hit by the tractor-trailer—

she's hell
      if you owe her
money—like

a bedbug-ridden
        family, who use
the grand piano

for a toilet
        and force you
to clean it out.

# On the Bicentennial

Empire half seas over, recessing—
haven't you got anything

sexier—once again be that young
nation who brought so much

happiness, let lips do what hands
do? And *off* she goes. Hands

of an overweight chimp, each finger
a thumb. The belle of the ball, standing

in the steam of a bakery line, gasping
like a radiator, circling from romance

to disillusionment—burdock,
heliotrope, hollyhock—in the field

behind the tractor-wagon stand
the unmagnificent quarter-horses

mortgaged among a distant knot
of snow—the cutpurse starlings speak and go

with better instruction. The romanticized
excitement of comfortable café

dwellers—proud men give themselves
to shapely goddesses and yielding

manly others. Water flows
over the land looking for rest, slewing

a skin of leaves, naked as a postcard—stars
hide your fire. We remain at your service.

# The Quiet Life

You is a pricy practical joke, a missed

    appointment, termination that didn't take,

doctor without depth, military march,

intolerant of mystery; a dinner party

    grope and stock exchange; growing aroused

in the shadow of compromise, in the pantry's

smell of lessening, of whatever

    comes along. You'll have him—

you can't have anything dripping

and no one to see, and should you

    be feared to share him your shrunk

chested enthusiasm, and shaven

gape—like a mouth ajar, an over-worn

    loafer—you'll liptongue and hand him,

poor spunk, half-screwed, like moth larva


rolling in a rice jar. To make nothing

    out of nothing but a backbend and take

three quarters of an hour over it.


No one ever captured the insanity

    of monologue like you did, vulgarizing

anger into irritation and a plaster


of panic, grinding fists into your eyes,

    like our child. So quiet now

it scrapes the calm from bones,

punctuated with involuntary

    exonerations, the house in weed,

shingles steaming, all fog


and submission, a celibate brothel

    (if nuns carried their duties

as you sexed, all saints they'd be.)


No, no solicitation in a park

    urinal, no sodomizing the duck

on account of its down, no slush


of thrushes in the rain gutter, no train

    of dangers, or snoring next door, eyes

unlit, half the sun and twice the rent.

# Love Letter from Edda Göring

Let's go eat somewhere
they can't see

what we're doing
under the table;

we'll chew the whale
to pieces,

and bowels tight
with happiness,

you can scream
"I'm the giant,

I'm the giant,"
if you're

ordered to.
Talking is safer

than sitting still.
It will be a bright

spring night,
the chestnut trees'

white blossoms
laying like dry skin

on the sidewalks,
stone lions covered

in astral light.
Electrical sighs

mourning the destruction
of thousands

of little machines
still

in working order.
We'll sweep the snow

into the sea
and I'll be

your monkey-woman;
you can watch

me bathe.
I'll believe

in anything
if you'll

believe in anything,
my often-too-late

little Pol Pot,
my catamite

with the bog-brown
eyes to sink into.

Then again, I can't
bear men—

their melancholy,
and annoying

thoroughness,
their resistance

to cleaning
the bathroom,

their knee-bends,
hoofs protruding

from their asses;
the battles

more boring
than horrible.

Men like this
make history.

An underpaid
accountant

and socialist,
human or something

of the sort,
I have a future

as a pacifist.
That I'm

still alive
proves nothing.

You're not
responsible

for the dark kid
horse-kicked

and folded
in the ditch. Still,

I'm worried
about something

but I'm not sure
what or why.

The sun hovering
flatly in the sky

unwilling to either
rise or set

you will stand
and walk off

toward the East
toward the war,

to search
for your regiment

once more. This time
you must try

and see
if you can succeed

in dying.
There's nothing,

you're not
capable of.

# Bricolage II

*After and for Molly Brodak, and after Timothy Donnelly*

People are wild and small and don't live very long.
The first to die are the ones who don't tell stories:

mouse masks and leaky chamber pots and pine
straw and red embroidery and the ugly song

a crow teaches her son so he can sleep.
They tilt their dark half dome eyes up for hawks:

the sky is open all the way; workers upright
on the line like spokes. Impossible dreams—

like building a birdhouse underwater. Dark pasts
are only good at coming back. Each day ahead

is lake black. The holy lies between things.
You hope you are remembering something

when you see it. Come back from there. If there is
no one else here. I'm not either. Half of me feels

strangled, a hard curve in a dirt road. I can't see
ahead. The last time I saw myself alive, I drew

the curtain back from the bed, stood by my sleeping
body. You will save yourself. You cannot help it.

# A Kind of Speech

*After Simone Muench*

These fragments, language,
my ruins. Like a blind

machine, a sea captain
who doesn't trust

the stars or the light
inside his skull, carried

off by an unsteady skiff
into the moon-swallowed

shadows. Words—dark
deciphering birds of flight,

a secret symmetry
restless in its syllable socket.

# Elegy

*After Simone Muench*

My shadow sleeps
with wolves

in an empty corner
of a house and whirling

snow. Shaking animal
life, bringing flame

from the other shore,
transformed in a howl.

This body at the edge
of breath with its

hundreds of corridors
so that when the time

comes there will be
this tongue that can

no longer pass
beyond its husk.

# Aubade

*After Simone Muench and Georgi Tenev*

Your fingers in my mouth
after slowly approaching

in the small hours
when tenderness seems

like good sleep. Place
a word in a hollow

where a hare could hide.
Alone together, ghostly

silhouettes accumulating
into a single body. It is

the human that is alien.
Still, I pass through you

as you pass through me.

# One Truth of Caring

*After Danielle Pafunda*

If you become a stream, run away,
my aunt told me. From then on, my body

was a card catalogue, the neighbor's

bed, a used car lot. She stenciled
her naked self with cats' eyes,

upholstered herself with maps

of the city's waterway. Put me in a vanity
drawer; supplied charcoals, pastels,

oil paints. I etched with my nails

into the wood rot. Within those confines
I grew a bridge of teak, and armory

with awnings. I finally emerged

when I felt the woman had died.
She hung in city hall against

a marble wall, like a lung, a gang

from a gallows. I took her down
against the advice of officials,

chaplains; put her in the vanity

drawer and climbed in after.
I drew an iron caisson, built

a dock from the silt up, a boathouse;

wrought a black wig, crocheted
a lace collar, and watched her run away

down our dock, tumble into quiet water.

# Being Alive May Come in Use

A hard face in soft sleep, it's a pity
he isn't a bit better looking. But

might be in time. Will her eyes rest
upon his vigorous hips? She will

perhaps eulogize him: I didn't know
he had died; sex with him was basically

the same, but the dishes began piling
up. His breath like a latrine soiled

by a small creature of the night
and hers: its mausoleum. Hard

to believe they were once teenagers
under a piano lying, nostrils-flared,

beside an ashtray. They liked standing
just at the edge of a subway platform

as an express train blew through. Heavy
words lightly thrown. But not to stand

on ship's deck and peer down into the heavy
water at a face in the fog, that was just the fog.

# An Ending

*After Mark Bibbins*


Rays burrowing in sand
like hearing someone typing

an endless suicide note
in a room at the end

of a carpeted hall, we go on
believing that nothing

can touch us here,
though loss is like

wearing a blouse made
of a thousand needles,

remembering the weight
of the phone in your hand

when the call came in,
the body a snowshoe hare

curled like a closed hand.

# A Bodily Way of Knowing

*After Mark Bibbins, Michael Dickman, and Joe Wenderoth*

We're the ancient
brides. It's so beautiful.

Even so I'm always glad
to get back home. To see

a man in handcuffs,
how you feel about that,

depends on whether
the servitude is voluntary.

People seem to respond
to what owns them. When

I first died I stole a lock
of your hair while you slept.

Now I dip it in ink, cross
my legs and squirm. And

on that final night I tore
eye-holes in a black pillowcase,

slipped it over my head,
made love to myself

in the mirror. We are
that animal everyone

is interested in but knows
almost nothing about. We

move out across the water
in our clumsy bodies

the color of steam
and blow out the breakers,

one by one, then hang
as moonless fish in river-rest

amid the vulnerability of hope.

# Shared Breath

*After Raul Zurita*

And like frozen hulls
our mouths appear

beneath icebergs
which float over the night

looking like strangled clothes;
the breath of our mouths

and those frozen exhalations
at sea amid frosted breakers.

The icebergs detach
and we are set loose,

gazing at the glaciers of the night.
And the frozen unknown

charcoal sky above revealed
the coast of a country

of snow covering the blue
membrane of the mountains,

and the sea still a blizzard
bordering the long beach

of meager love; the unknown
calling to us in which we must

look like children now,
returning the bluish gaze

as if in a trance, as if finally
a square hatchway revealed

a piece of welcome sky
and the frosted hills of the waves.

# Elegy II

House passing
through night

snow, keeping
our secrets, stalled

in forgetfulness:
a hollow place

where no one goes
anymore, endless

corridors, blacked out
garden lights, the bored

forest and cancelled
stars, two hounds baying

frozen from a loss
of love, the face

I made for you.

# Translocation

Sternal notch,
coastal headland.

She walked
into the ocean.

Didn't want
to die. Just

couldn't tell where
the horizon was.

# Bricolage

*After and for Molly Brodak*


To be alive means to be separated by a boundary—
love can kind of thin out if stretched too far

between then and now like a portraiture
of weather push-pinned to a map. The past cools

and hardens, and now that's all there was.
And an entire person is wasted on introspection—

in the background of insignificant action. You'll never
find the past. When you do find it, you'll see

no one's there. Not even the you you still hope
to meet. Landforms are about erosion. The piers

of a port, the spikes of cranes slicing the sky, the labyrinth
of docks, the dark silhouettes of cargo ships, the sea's

snowstorm covering the blue mountains. And the icebergs
floating through the night, like stranded clouds bruised

purple from the coming dawn. I still don't know the world,
only how it appears to me and looking has made me sick,

holding my lamp of knowing on the rim, and looking in.
One shadow overtakes another. I already knew

the ending. I used all of myself, all of the self given
to me, all of it. I'm here, I'm here is all it says.

And it's helpless, my body. My swifts are flightless.

# About the Author

Adam Day is the author of *Left-Handed Wolf* (LSU Press, 2020), and of *Model of a City in Civil War* (Sarabande Books, 2015), and the recipient of a Poetry Society of America Chapbook Fellowship for *Badger, Apocrypha,* and of a PEN Award. His work has appeared in *APR, Boston Review, The Progressive, Southern Review, Kenyon Review, Fence,* and elsewhere. He is the publisher of *Action, Spectacle.*

www.ingramcontent.com/pod-product-compliance
Lightning Source LLC
Chambersburg PA
CBHW030912170426
43193CB00009BA/822